Pebble® Plus

Wonderful World of Reading

Reading Is Everywhere

by Martha E. H. Rustad

Consulting Editor: Gail Saunders-Smith, PhD

Consultant: JoAnne DeLurey Reed, Librarian and Teacher
Scroggins Elementary School, Houston, Texas

CAPSTONE PRESS
a capstone imprint

Pebble Plus Books are published by Capstone Press,
1710 Roe Crest Drive, North Mankato, Minnesota 56003.
www.capstonepub.com

Library of Congress Cataloging-in-Publication Data
Rustad, Martha E. H. (Martha Elizabeth Hillman), 1975–
 Reading is everywhere / by Martha E.H. Rustad.
    pages cm.—(Pebble plus. Wonderful world of reading)
 Includes bibliographical references and index.
 ISBN 978-1-62065-096-7 (library binding)
 ISBN 978-1-4765-1746-9 (eBook PDF)
1. Books and reading—Juvenile literature. 2. Labels—Juvenile literature. 3. Signs and signboards—Juvenile literature. I. Title.
 Z1003.R96 2013
 028.9—dc23
                                                  2012030348

Editorial Credits
Erika L. Shores, editor; Veronica Scott, designer; Marcie Spence, media researcher; Laura Manthe, production specialist

Photo Credits
Alamy Images: Chris Rout, 7, Marmaduke St. John, 11; Capstone Studio: Karon Dubke, cover (child), 13; Corbis: Sylvain Sonnet, 15; Shutterstock: amenic181, 5 (child), Andrey Bayda, cover (background), CandyBox Images, 19, jorisvo, 5 (background), SandiMako, 21, Tan Hung Meng, 17, Tyler Olson, 9

Note to Parents and Teachers

The Wonderful World of Reading series supports Common Core State Standards for Language Arts related to craft and structure, to text types and writing purpose, and to research for building and presenting knowledge. This book describes and illustrates common places where written words are found. The images support early readers in understanding the text. The repetition of words and phrases helps early readers learn new words. This book also introduces early readers to subject-specific vocabulary words, which are defined in the Glossary section. Early readers may need assistance to read some words and to use the Table of Contents, Glossary, Read More, Internet Sites, and Index sections of the book.

Printed in the United States of America in North Mankato, Minnesota.
092012   006933CGS13

TABLE OF CONTENTS

Looking for Words

We read words in books.

But where else do

we find words?

Reading is everywhere!

At Home

In the kitchen, read labels

on cans. What are

the soup's ingredients?

In the living room,

read directions for

a computer game.

At School

In the classroom,

read the poem

on the board.

Dragon Poem

I wish I had a dragon
With diamond-studded scales,
With claws like silver sabers,
And fangs like silver nails,
A dragon fierce and faithful,
Always ready by my side,
A dragon to defend me
Or to take me for a ride.

By Jack

In the library, find books

for a report.

See the nonfiction books

sitting on the shelves.

Juvenile
NonFiction
001 - 394.268 ➡
⬅ 394.269 - 551.499

Out and About

On a busy city street,

look at a subway sign.

Read all the billboards.

At the zoo, signs tell

where the animals are.

Which way to

the polar bears?

Gibbon

长臂猿 テナガザル

Orang Utan

人猿 オランウータン

Polar Bear

北极熊 ホッキョクグマ

Wild Africa

非洲原野 ワイルドアフリカ

Fragile Forest

脆弱森林 フラジャイルフォレスト

Guanaco

美洲驼 グアナコ

Sun Bear

马来熊 マレーグマ

Camel

骆驼 ラクダ

Maned Wolf

鬃狼 タテガミオオカミ

At the grocery store,

read the signs for

the many kinds

of bread.

Words tell us stories.

Words tell us information.

Words are everywhere!

DIVE SHOP →

DIGITAL PHOTO CENTER →

CLASS ROOM ►►

ACTIVITY CENTER ►►

TRAINING CENTER ►►

Glossary

billboard—a large outdoor sign used to tell people about goods or services

directions—instructions that tell how to do something

ingredient—something that goes into a mixture

label—a piece of paper, cloth, or plastic that is attached to something and gives information about it

poem—a piece of writing set out in short lines that often rhyme

nonfiction—books that tell facts that are true

subway—a train that travels in a tunnel underground

Read More

Banks, Kate. *Max's Words.* New York: Farrar, Straus and Giroux, 2006.

Kawa, Katie. *My First Trip to the Library.* My First Adventures. New York: Gareth Stevens Pub., 2012.

Lyons, Shelly. *Signs in My Neighborhood.* My Neighborhood. North Mankato, Minn.: Capstone Press, 2013.

Internet Sites

FactHound offers a safe, fun way to find Internet sites related to this book. All of the sites on FactHound have been researched by our staff.

Here's all you do:

Visit *www.facthound.com*

Type in this code: 9781620650967

Super-cool stuff!
Check out projects, games and lots more at
www.capstonekids.com

23

Index

Word Count: 117
Grade: 1
Early-Intervention Level: 19